TOOLS FOR CAREGIVERS

- **F&P LEVEL:** A
- **WORD COUNT:** 28
- **CURRICULUM CONNECTIONS:** reptiles, fish, colors

Skills to Teach

- **HIGH-FREQUENCY WORDS:** I, see
- **CONTENT WORDS:** blue, gray, green, orange, red, scales, yellow
- **PUNCTUATION:** exclamation point, periods
- **WORD STUDY:** /k/, spelled c (*scales*); long /a/, spelled ay (*gray*); long /e/, spelled ee (*green*, *see*); long /o/, spelled ow (*yellow*); /oo/, spelled ue (*blue*)
- **TEXT TYPE:** information report

Before Reading Activities

- Read the title and give a simple statement of the main idea.
- Have students "walk" through the book and talk about what they see in the pictures.
- Introduce new vocabulary by having students predict the first letter and locate the word in the text.
- Discuss any unfamiliar concepts that are in the text.

After Reading Activities

The reptiles and fish in the book have different colored scales. Print out coloring sheets of different reptiles and fish for the readers to color. After all are colored, ask readers to sort them by color. Then arrange them in the order of the rainbow.

Tadpole Books are published by Jump!, 5357 Penn Avenue South, Minneapolis, MN 55419, www.jumplibrary.com

Copyright ©2023 Jump. International copyright reserved in all countries. No part of this book may be reproduced in any form without written permission from the publisher.

Editor: Jenna Gleisner **Designer:** Molly Ballanger

Photo Credits: Nynke van Holten/Shutterstock, cover; Eric Isselee/Shutterstock, 1; Miropa/iStock, 2tl, 14–15; Rocksweeper/Shutterstock, 2tr, 4–5; Daniel MR/Shutterstock, 2ml, 12–13; Lotus_studio/Shutterstock, 2mr, 8–9; Dushyant Kumar Thakur/iStock, 2bl, 6–7; Lauren Suryanata/Shutterstock, 2br, 10–11; Photoshot - NHPA/SuperStock, 3; Shutterstock, 16.

Library of Congress Cataloging-in-Publication Data
Names: Gleisner, Jenna Lee, author.
Title: Scales / by Jenna Lee Gleisner.
Description: Minneapolis, MN: Jump!, Inc., (2023)
Series: I see animal textures! | Includes index.
Audience: Ages 3–6
Identifiers: LCCN 2022011573 (print)
LCCN 2022011574 (ebook)
ISBN 9798885240444 (hardcover)
ISBN 9798885240451 (paperback)
ISBN 9798885240468 (ebook)
Subjects: LCSH: Scales (Fishes)—Juvenile literature.
Classification: LCC QL639 .G54 2023 (print) | LCC QL639 (ebook) | DDC 597.147/7—dc23/eng/20220328
LC record available at https://lccn.loc.gov/2022011573
LC ebook record available at https://lccn.loc.gov/2022011574

I SEE ANIMAL TEXTURES!
SCALES

by Jenna Lee Gleisner

TABLE OF CONTENTS

Words to Know 2

Scales 3

Let's Review! 16

Index 16

SCALES

scale

I see scales.

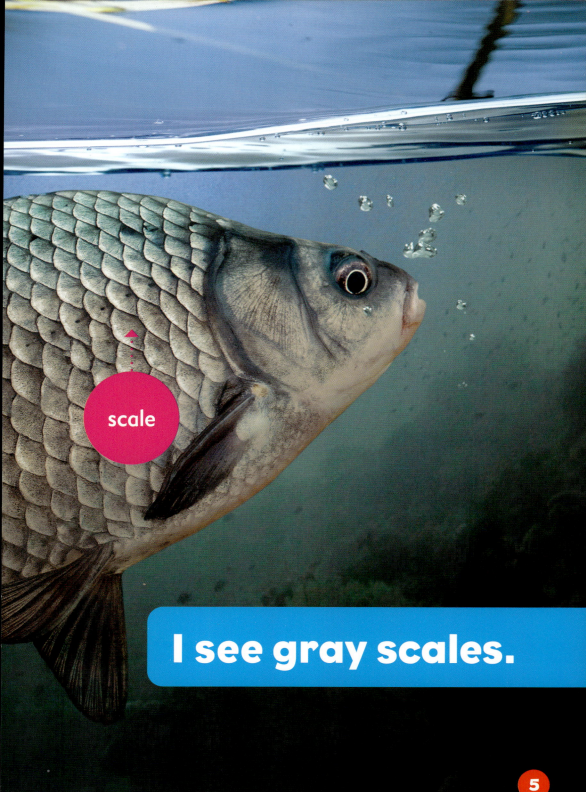

scale

I see gray scales.

I see orange scales.

scale

I see yellow scales.

I see green scales.

LET'S REVIEW!

Scales are flat pieces of hard skin. Reptiles and fish have scales. What kinds of scales do you see below?

INDEX

blue 15

gray 5

green 13

orange 9

red 7

yellow 11